ICE CREAM

ICE CREAM COOK BOOK

by Earl Goldman

Illustrations from the turn of the century by Mike Nelson, with an assist from Craig Torlucci.

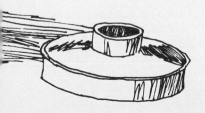

A Nitty Gritty Book*
Published by
Nitty Gritty Productions
P.O. Box 5457
Concord, California 94524

*Nitty Gritty Books - Trademark
Owned by Nitty Gritty Productions
Concord, California

ISBN 0-911954-09-0

books designed with giving in mind

Make It Ahead French
Soups & Stews
Kid's Pets Book
Crepes & Omelets
Microwave Cooking
Vegetable Cookbook
Kid's Arts and Crafts
Bread Baking
The Crockery Pot Cookbook
Kid's Garden Book
Classic Greek Cooking

The Compleat American
  Housewife 1776
Low Carbohydrate Cookbook
Kid's Cookbook
Italian
Cheese Guide & Cookbook
Miller's German
Quiche & Souffle
To My Daughter, With Love
Natural Foods
Chinese Vegetarian
Jewish Gourmet

Working Couples
Mexican
Sunday Breakfast
Fisherman's Wharf Cookbook
Ice Cream Cookbook
Hippo Hamburger
Blender Cookbook
The Wok, a Chinese Cookbook
Cast Iron Cookbook
Japanese Country
Fondue Cookbook

from nitty gritty productions

TABLE OF CONTENTS

Credit for the first frozen dessert is given by some historians to Nero Claudius Caesar, emperor of Rome (54—68 A.D.). Actually, it was made with snow that he ordered brought him from the mountains to which he added fruit juices and other flavorings. The result was probably not unlike the modern day snow cone. Because of the difficulty of getting and keeping ice, only the emperor could afford this newly discovered luxury.

A second theory holds that the Chinese were the first to learn of the pleasure of frozen desserts and that they eventually revealed their secret recipe to Marco Polo. In the 13th century he wrote of the Chinese "water ices" upon his return from one of his journeys. Marco Polo apparently added milk to these ices and thus created a frozen dessert much closer to the ice cream we know.

Water ices are reported to have been brought to France from Italy by Catherine de Medici, the child bride of King Henry II, in 1550.

She delighted guests in her court with her own recipes based on that of Marco Polo. Her son, Henry III, was said to eat ices every day.

The first ice cream was created by Jacques, a French chef to the court of Charles I of England in 1640. He called it "cream ice". The frozen dessert swept the courts of Europe and for many years was the favorite dessert for nobility.

It is also said that soon afterward they were made in Paris by a M. Contreaux, an Italian. More definite records, however, date back to the year 1660 when an Italian cook named Procopio Cultelli from Palermo established his "Cafe Procope," where for the first time ice cream was made available to the common man. This practice soon spread to other Parisian eateries.

It is said that ice cream was introduced next to England from France by Carlo Gatti and was served at the court of King Charles I.

The earliest printed record of cream ices is found in "The Ex-

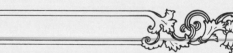

perienced English Housekeeper," by Elizabeth Raffald, published in the year 1769. A French cook named Clermont published a book in London in 1776 containing recipes for making sweet-ices. There are English cookbooks over 150 years old that contain recipes for cream ices. The early English cream ices were made of milk, sugar, eggs, arrowroot or flour, and flavoring—not unlike our present day ice cream.

Ice cream apparently made its way to the New World not long after. A guest at the home of William Bladen, the governor of Maryland at the beginning of the 18th century, wrote: "We had a dessert no less curious; among the rarities of which it was compos'd was some fine Ice Cream, which, with Strawberries and Milk, eat Most Deliciously."

The first ice cream advertisement appeared in a New York newspaper, "The Post Boy," on June 8, 1786, and read "Ladies and Gentlemen may be supplied with ice cream every day at the City Tavern by their humble servant Joseph Crowe."

INTRODUCTION

The first ice cream parlor in America was owned and operated by an imaginative man named Hall. It was located on Chatham Street in New York. We would like to be able to report that Mr. Hall went on to open several hundred franchised stores, but he was soon copied by many others and ice cream parlors sprang up throughout New York City. George Washington was so delighted with the ice cream he tasted at Mr. Hall's establishment that he later bought a "cream machine for making ice." Mt. Vernon was equipped with two pewter ice cream pots.

In fact, ice cream seems to have been a favorite of many of our founding fathers. Thomas Jefferson learned recipes while he was in France. He served Meringue Glacée and Baked Alaska at many of his state dinners.

Ice cream might not have been so popular among our early statesmen had they not had servants to prepare it for them. The process was time-consuming and quite tiring. It demanded great perseverance as

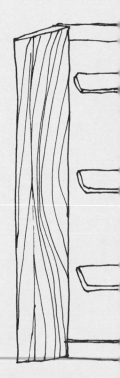

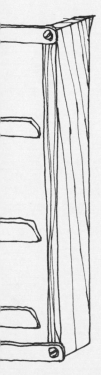

well as patience, for none of the equipment was mechanized. The ingredients for the ice cream were placed in a metal container which was then placed in a wooden bucket filled with ice. These ingredients then had to be beaten by hand. The bucket was then shaken back and forth until the ice cream solidified. This process remained unchanged until well into the 19th century. In 1846 an American woman named Nancy Johnson invented an ice cream freezer with a new rotary element called a "dasher." The dasher was connected to an outside handle. As this handle was rotated it caused the dasher to whip the ingredients, which kept them creamy and smooth during the freezing process. The present day home ice cream freezer, whether hand-cranked or electric, operates on this same principle.

Even after ice cream had become a favorite of the common man as well as the wealthy, it remained for many years exclusively a home-made product. The invention of larger units and improved cranking

methods made possible the first ice cream "industry." Jacob Fussel, a Baltimore dairyman, opened the first factory in 1851 in Washington, D.C.

Mr. Fussell at first decided to manufacture ice cream in order to use up his surplus cream. He sold his ice cream for 60 cents a quart. He soon found the manufacture of ice cream to be far more profitable than dealing in milk. That is when he devoted his entire plant to the making of this new product. In 1862 he added another plant in Boston, and in 1864 he opened another in New York. The average price was then set at $1.25 a quart.

Today, prepackaged ice cream is available in every supermarket and corner store. Its quality varies from weak ice milk products to rich, ultra-smooth catering quality. However, the latter is extremely difficult to find, even in large cities, and is simply not available in most parts of America.

With the help of this book, you will be able to make at home ice creams and sherbets of superior quality and flavor to delight your family and friends. And, what is more, you will be able to save money as well. Homemade ice creams and sherbets always cost less than their store-bought counterparts if the comparison is made by weight. (Normally the homemade product weighs at least twice as much simply because it contains less air.) A third and most important advantage is that making ice cream at home is a great deal of fun!

TYPES OF "ICE CREAM"

There are many different types of "ice cream." In general, ice cream is a frozen cream and milk product with sweetening and flavorings added. There are, however, many variations on this product.

Ice milk is a product similar to ice cream but it contains less milk fat and total milk solids. It is often sold in its soft state at roadside refreshment stands under the name of "frostie" or "softie."

Frozen custard or French ice cream is a frozen product in which eggs or egg yolks are added to the usual ice cream ingredients to make a richer result.

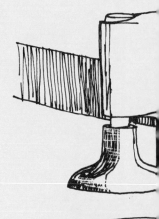

Sherbet is made of milk or milk and cream. Sweeteners, fruit or fruit juices, water, flavorings, and stabilizers may also be added. The number of calories is slightly less than that contained by ice cream. Sherbets have twice the amount of sugar as ice cream.

Mousse is a frozen dessert made of sweetened, flavored whipped cream or thin cream and gelatine.

eight

Fruit ices are made by using fruit, fruit juices, water and sweeteners—no milk. Many of the flavorings that are used for sherbet are also added.

Mellorine or diet or imitation ice cream is a frozen dessert made with vegetable fats such as cottonseed or soybean oil, rather than with milk fats. Since vegetable fats do not require refrigeration for storage, mellorine is less expensive to produce than ice cream made with milk fats. Sale is regulated by state laws and permitted in only 14 states.

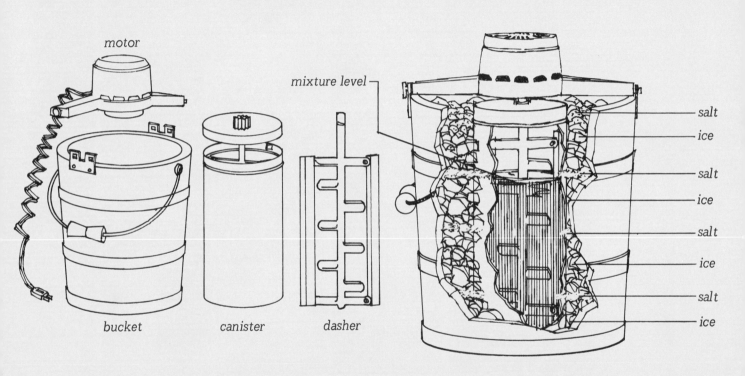

motor

mixture level

salt
ice
salt
ice
salt
ice
salt
ice

bucket   canister   dasher

Ice cream freezers are a fairly standard product. The typical maker consists of a two gallon bucket made of wood, plastic, or fiberglass into which a one gallon ice cream canister is placed. The canister contains a dasher which remains still while the canister turns. The wooden bucket is the old standard, as it is probably the most durable. However, it has one major drawback. It must be soaked in water for several hours before use so that the staves will swell, otherwise it will leak like a sieve.

The regular plastic bucket is acceptable; however, it is not particularly durable, and is relatively poorly insulated.

Fiberglass is extremely strong and long lasting, and if it is reasonably thick, it should prove to be both durable and a good insulating material.

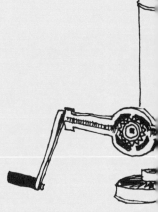

The canisters are similar in most freezers. The ones with the see-through plastic covers are particularly nice, because they allow the user to see the mix harden.

Electric mixers are easier to use than hand cranked models and are well worth their added cost; however, one drawback is that they cannot be used for campouts and picnics where there is no electricity. The hand crank models are also fun for the kids, although most modern day children soon tire of cranking.

As is true with most products with a long useful life, the reader would be advised well to spend a little more and get the highest quality model that his budget will allow.

FREEZER INSTRUCTIONS

Whether you are using an electric or hand cranked model, the following instructions should produce consistent results when making ice cream or sherbet:

(1) Always scald the inner canister and beaters with boiling water. Simply pour boiling water into the canister with the dasher in place, and then pour it off.

(2) Pour the chilled mixture through a fine mesh strainer into the canister, using a wooden spoon to force the mixture through the mesh. Or, if you prefer, you may use your blender to smooth the chilled mixture. Place the canister in the refrigerator to chill overnight if desired—although not really necessary, this helps make a smoother ice cream.

(3) After chilling the mixture, place the dasher in the canister, put the cover in place, and place the canister in the bucket. If the

bucket is made of wood, it should have been soaked in water the night before so that its wooden sides will expand to prevent leakage. This is, of course, unnecessary with plastic or fiberglass buckets.

(4) Ice should be chopped up into small coarse pieces. One can buy crushed ice, use an ice crusher (coarse setting), or simply place large pieces in an old burlap bag, or pillow case, and use a hammer to crush them. The smaller the pieces, the more actual ice (by weight) you will be able to put in the bucket. However, because small pieces have more surface area than large pieces, they will melt faster. So adjust the size to your particular needs. Always have plenty of ice on hand. It usually requires 25 lbs. of ice to make a gallon of ice cream. While you are at it, you can make two 1-gallon batches with the same amount of ice.

(5) Salt is used because salt causes ice to melt faster. The larger the

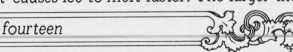

proportion of salt used in relation to the ice, the faster the ice will melt. No harm can possibly be done by adding too little salt. You can always add more. However, if you add too much salt, you will cause your mix to freeze too quickly, and your resulting ice cream will not be smooth.

Simply place about three inches of crushed ice in the bucket with the canister in place, then add about two handfuls of salt. Then add three more inches of ice, then two more handfuls of salt. When the ice salt mixture is just below the top of the canister, you can plug in the electric mixer, or start cranking the hand operated one.

(6) Keep cranking steadily until the mixture thickens. With a hand operated model, keep cranking until you can't crank any longer. With an electric model, pull the plug when the motor starts to

labor. *If the mixture does not thicken after 20 minutes, just pour off some of the water through the drain hole and then add two or three more handfuls of salt and another layer of ice.*

(7) *Remove the canister from the bucket and wipe the outside of the canister dry with a towel to remove all traces of salt. Remove the dasher and sample your luscious frozen delicacy. Then place several layers of wax paper over the ice cream. Replace the canister cover and place the canister back into the bucket. Pour the excess water off and add sufficient layers of ice and salt to fill the bucket. Place a stack of newspapers of top for insulation and set ice cream aside to cure for at least three hours. If you have a good home freezer that maintains a temperature of $0°$ or thereabouts, you can remove the ice cream from the canister immediately, place it in freezer containers, and let it cure for several hours in your home freezer. You can then make addition-*

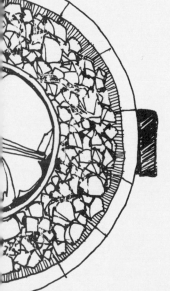

al batches of ice cream or sherbet in your ice cream freezer. Remember that on hot days, freezers do not work as efficiently as you might think. 0 degrees is not often attained by home quality electric refrigerator-freezers. However, the old fashioned method is simple and it always works.

(8) After you and your guests have had your fill, you can spoon the extra ice cream into freezer containers for storage. Don't be surprised if the ice cream gets extremely hard in your freezer and has to be softened before being served. This is a characteristic of the homemade product, as it is very dense. One quart of homemade ice cream weighs about the same as two quarts of commercial ice cream.

All of the recipes in this book are designed to make four quarts of ice cream or sherbet. This requires three quarts of mix. The balance will be air, whipped into the mixture by the beaters.

Once you have tried a particular recipe, make a note on the page as to your personal taste to guide you in the amount of flavoring and sugar to use the next time you make it.

Do not judge the taste of the ice cream by the taste of the mix before freezing, the coldness of the frozen product dulls the taste buds. For this reason, the mix will always taste overly sweet and flavorful before freezing.

ICE CREAM WITHOUT AN ICE CREAM FREEZER

All of the recipes in this book may be made in the ice cube trays of your refrigerator. However, the results will not be as smooth, and the use of an ice cream freezer is strongly recommended.

If you do not have one, simply make one-fourth of the recipe called for, and freeze it in your ice cube trays until it is mushy. Then remove the partially frozen mix from the trays and beat it with an electric mixer until it is smooth. Then pour it back into the trays and freeze until solid. It is practically impossible to avoid crystals from forming; however, many people find this method satisfactory.

A recipe for a low calorie ice milk using non-fat milk and an artificial low calorie sweetener is given on page 33. Using this recipe as a base, any of the flavors in this book can be added. Naturally, it is best if relatively low calorie flavorings are used.

In most cases, the tastiest low calorie desserts which one can make are the sherbets. Simply substitute an equivalent amount of artificial sweetener for the sugar in the sherbet recipes.

Please remember that sugar helps to make the dessert keep in the freezer. Low calorie desserts made without sugar should be consumed within a few days after preparation.

VANILLA RECIPES ARE BASIC

The following vanilla ice cream recipes vary from ultra-rich catering quality ice cream using eggs and cream to inexpensive low calorie ice milk using non-fat milk.

They form the basic ingredient for all of the flavored ice cream recipes which follow.

First select the vanilla recipe that suits the occasion (and your pocketbook). Then add a flavor from the flavored section. This way, you have a choice of many different qualities of ice cream for whatever flavor you select.

VANILLA CUSTARD ICE CREAM

1 quart plus 3 cups whole milk
12 egg yolks
2 tsp. salt
3 cups sugar
1 quart whipping cream
4 T. vanilla or 3 - 2" vanilla beans crushed in a blender

Scald milk in a large 6 quart saucepan. In a large bowl, beat together egg yolks and salt. Add about 3 cups of the hot milk to the egg yolks slowly while stirring constantly. Then return this mixture to the milk in the pan. Add sugar and keep stirring while cooking at medium heat. When mixture coats the spoon or just starts to boil, remove from heat. In most cases, the mixture will be lumpy. Don't worry. Just remember to strain it. Chill. Stir in whipping cream and vanilla and freeze.

VANILLA CUSTARD ICE CREAM

This is a delicious catering quality custard ice cream. Please notice that it uses a ratio of approximately 2 parts milk to 1 part of cream. By substituting additional cream for some of the milk, it can be made even richer.

You will have lots of left over egg whites. Use them for Baked Alaska, Lemon Milk Sherbet, or make meringue shells. They are delicious filled with ice cream and topped with fresh berries or peaches.

VANILLA ICE CREAM

This is pure vanilla ice cream with no eggs added. It has a very clean, fresh taste, but it is not quite as smooth as custard ice cream. It is very rich. Delicious with black coffee.

3 quarts light cream
3 cups sugar
1 tsp. salt
4 tsp. vanilla

Dissolve the sugar in one cup of the cream. Add the remaining ingredients. Chill the mixture, and freeze.

FRENCH VANILLA ICE CREAM

2 quarts plus 3 cups light cream
6 eggs, beaten
3 cups sugar
1 tsp. salt
4 T. vanilla extract

Combine ingredients. Chill in refrigerator before freezing.

PHILADELPHIA VANILLA ICE CREAM

3 envelopes clear gelatine
1 1/2 quarts whole milk
1 1/2 quarts light cream
3 cups sugar
4 tsp. vanilla
1 tsp. salt

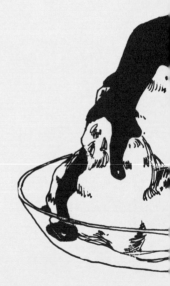

Pour one cup of cold milk in a bowl and sprinkle gelatine on top. Stir thoroughly. Scald the remaining milk and add gelatine-milk mixture to it. Add sugar, and chill. Place mixture in canister, add cream, salt, and vanilla. Freeze.

HALF-HALF VANILLA ICE CREAM

3 quarts half and half
3 cups sugar
4 T. vanilla
2 tsp. salt

Heat one quart of half and half almost to the boiling point and dissolve sugar and salt in it. Add remaining half and half and vanilla, chill and then freeze.

VANILLA PUDDING ICE CREAM

2 quarts milk
2 cups light corn syrup
2 boxes vanilla pudding mix
2 tsp. vanilla extract
2 tsp. almond extract
2 cups heavy cream

Add milk and corn syrup to pudding powder and cook over low heat until thickened, stirring constantly. Chill. Add flavorings and heavy cream. Pour into canister and freeze.

VANILLA JUNKET ICE CREAM

2 quarts milk
2 cups whipping cream
2 cups sugar
4 T. vanilla
4 T. cold water
4 junket tablets

Dissolve junket tablets in cold water. Mix milk, sugar and salt and heat to lukewarm. Add water and junket mixture, chill, add cream and vanilla and freeze.

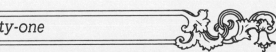

MARSHMALLOW VANILLA ICE CREAM

In this recipe, marshmallows serve as the binder and thickening agent.

2 1/2 quarts evaporated milk
60 regular sized marshmallows
1 1/2 cups sugar
4 T. vanilla
2 tsp. salt

Dissolve marshmallows and sugar in 1 quart of milk and heat almost to boiling point. Add remaining milk, salt, and vanilla. Chill before adding to the canister to freeze.

LOW CALORIE VANILLA ICE CREAM

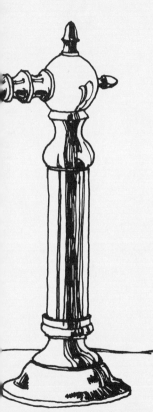

6 eggs
5 cups of milk
12 saccharin tablets (1/2 grain)
    or 4 T. liquid sweetener
6 1/2 cups half and half
3 T. plain gelatin
4 T. vanilla
3/4 tsp. salt

Make a custard of the eggs, milk, and liquid sweetener. Soak the gelatin in a small amount of water and add enough hot custard to dissolve the gelatin. Cool. Add cream, vanilla, salt and gelatin to custard. Strain and freeze. This will still be palatable and contain even fewer calories if all of the milk and half and half are replaced by non-fat milk.

VANILLA CUSTARD ICE MILK

3 envelopes clear gelatin
3 quarts plus 2 cups milk
3 cups sugar
6 eggs
4 tsp. vanilla
1 T. salt

Put one cup of the cold milk aside in a bowl and sprinkle the gelatin on top of it and stir thoroughly. Make a custard of the remaining milk, yolks of the eggs, sugar and salt. Add gelatin milk mixture to the hot custard and stir until dissolved. When cold, add flavoring. Just before freezing, add egg whites, beaten stiff.

VANILLA EVAPORATED ICE MILK

3 quarts (6 cans) evaporated milk
3 T. vanilla
2 tsp. salt
3 cups sugar

Dissolve the sugar in 2 quarts of milk and heat almost to the boiling point. Remove from heat. Chill, add remaining ingredients and freeze.

This is an inexpensive base for a strongly flavored ice cream such as chocolate.

Normally, commercially made vanilla ice creams are slightly richer in butterfat content than their flavored counterparts. This is because the flavorings cost money, and something (the extra butterfat) must be taken out to make up for the added cost of the flavorings.

In making your own ice cream, you are not limited by cost considerations, and you can select a rich, expensive vanilla recipe for your base and have the finest flavored ice cream you've ever experienced.

As a general rule, always use a flavoring with poor quality, less costly vanillas, so that the flavoring can mask the lower quality. When you make vanilla ice cream, make the richest that you can afford.

All of the following flavorings can be used with any of the preceding vanilla recipes.

STRAWBERRIES AND CREAM

3 quarts fresh, ripe strawberries
1 cup sugar
A vanilla recipe from pages 24 through 35

Hull and clean and quarter the strawberries. Sugar them and then fold into your favorite vanilla ice cream when it is completed but still rather soft. This method keeps the flavor and the color of the berries and ice cream separate. A wonderful summertime treat.

STRAWBERRY ICE CREAM

1 cup sugar

6 cups fresh ripe strawberries

A vanilla recipe from pages 24 through 35

Add the additional cup of sugar to the vanilla recipe. Crush berries in a collander. Add berries to the vanilla ice cream mix just before freezing. For a redder color, add a few drops of red food coloring.

CHOCOLATE ICE CREAM

1 cup sugar
4 squares cooking chocolate
A vanilla recipe from pages 24 through 35

    Dissolve chocolate in milk or cream when heating ingredients in vanilla recipe. Add extra cup of sugar to sugar in vanilla recipe. Use more or less chocolate to taste.

    For Rocky Road Ice Cream, add 4 cups miniature marshmallows and 1 cup chopped nutmeats.

BITTERSWEET CHOCOLATE ICE CREAM

5 squares cooking chocolate
A vanilla recipe from pages 24 through 35

    Dissolve chocolate in milk or cream when heating ingredients in vanilla recipe. Use more or less chocolate to taste.

COFFEE ICE CREAM

6 T. Instant coffee
A vanilla recipe from pages 24 through 35

   Add 6 T. instant coffee to the hot mix of any of the vanilla recipes. Add more coffee if a stronger taste is desired. Remember it will not taste quite so strong after it is frozen.

CARAMEL ICE CREAM

3 cups granulated sugar
1 1/2 cups hot water
A vanilla recipe from pages 24 through 35

Place 1 1/2 cups sugar in a saucepan over a hot fire and stir until sugar is melted and the color of maple syrup. Add 1 1/2 cups hot water and simmer until the consistency of hot syrup. Add another 1 1/2 cups sugar and dissolve. Use this mixture in place of 3 cups of sugar in your favorite vanilla ice cream recipe.

PISTACHIO ICE CREAM

1 lb. pistachio nuts
green food coloring
A vanilla recipe from pages 24 through 35

Blanch one pound of pistachio nuts. Chop finely, or pound in a mortar. Add to your favorite vanilla ice cream recipe just before freezing. Add a small amount of green coloring. This is particularly nice for the holiday season.

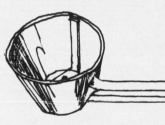

ORANGE ICE CREAM

2 cans frozen concentrated orange juice
A vanilla recipe from pages 24 through 35

    Thaw juice and pour into cannister with vanilla ice cream mix. This is preferable to using fresh juice, since less water is added and the resulting mixture is richer.

PEPPERMINT STICK ICE CREAM

1 1/2 lbs. peppermint stick candy
A vanilla recipe from pages 24 through 35
2 cups milk

Crush or grind 1 1/2 lbs. peppermint stick candy. Soak in the refrigerator overnight in 2 cups of milk. Substitute this milk-candy mixture for 2 cups of milk in your favorite vanilla ice cream recipe.

TUTTI-FRUTTI ICE CREAM

1 1/2 lbs. assorted candied fruit

A vanilla recipe from pages 24 through 35

When your favorite vanilla ice cream is half frozen, add 1 1/2 lbs. of candied fruit—equal parts of peaches, apricots, cherries, pineapple, and pears—all cut fine. Mix well and finish freezing.

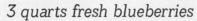

BLUEBERRY ICE CREAM

3 quarts fresh blueberries
1 cup sugar
1 cup water
A vanilla recipe from pages 24 through 35

   Simmer berries in sugar and water until soft. Allow to cool and force through sieve. Add to vanilla ice cream mix and freeze.

BLUEBERRIES AND CREAM

3 quarts fresh blueberries
3 cups sugar
A vanilla recipe from pages 24 through 35

      Sugar berries well and set aside. After they have absorbed the sugar, fold them into your favorite vanilla ice cream after it is completed but still rather soft. This method preserves the whole berries inside of the ice cream.

2 cans frozen concentrate lemon or lime juice
or 1 can of each for lemon-lime.
A vanilla recipe from pages 24 through 35

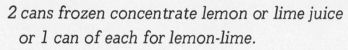

Thaw juice and pour into cannister with vanilla ice cream mixture.

The use of frozen concentrate is preferable to fresh juice because less water is added and the resulting mixture is richer.

MANGO ICE CREAM

6 *cups ripe mango pulp*
A vanilla recipe from pages 24 through 35

Add six cups of ripe mango pulp to your favorite vanilla ice cream when it is half frozen and continue freezing.

RUM RAISIN ICE CREAM

3 cups seedless raisins
3/4 cup rum
A vanilla recipe from pages 24 through 35

Grind the raisins in a meat grinder and then soak them in the rum. Fold rum-raisin mixture into any of the vanilla ice cream recipes when partially frozen. For variety, add 2 cups of chopped walnuts or pecans.

MOCHA ICE CREAM

3 bags of semi-sweet chocolate bits
6 T. instant coffee
A vanilla recipe from pages 24 through 35

Melt chocolate in double boiler and add it along with coffee to hot mixture in vanilla recipe.

CHERRY ICE CREAM

3 boxes of fresh cherries
1 cup sugar
A vanilla recipe from pages 24 through 35

Pit and quarter the cherries and cover with the sugar. Let stand. Add to your favorite vanilla ice cream recipe when it is half frozen. Add a small amount of red food coloring if desired. Or you can fold the cherries into the frozen completed ice cream. If you would prefer to use canned cherries, use 3 cans and do not sugar them.

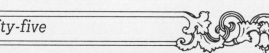

RASPBERRY ICE CREAM

1 cup sugar
6 cups fresh ripe raspberries
A vanilla recipe from pages 24 through 35

Add the additional cup of sugar to the vanilla recipe. Crush berries in collander. Add berries to vanilla ice cream mix just before freezing. For a redder color, add a few drops of red food coloring.

1 cup sugar
6 cups fresh ripe raspberries
A vanilla recipe from pages 24 through 35

Sugar the raspberries and then fold into the vanilla ice cream when it is completed, but still soft. This method results in vanilla ice cream containing whole fresh raspberries.

PEACH ICE CREAM

4 cups crushed ripe peaches
1/2 cup sugar
A vanilla recipe from pages 24 through 35

Add additional sugar to vanilla ice cream recipe. When vanilla ice cream is almost frozen, add peaches.

FRESH APRICOT RIPPLE ICE CREAM

4 cups crushed ripe apricots
1/2 cup sugar
A vanilla recipe from pages 24 through 35

Add additional sugar to vanilla ice cream recipe. When vanilla ice cream is almost frozen, add apricots.

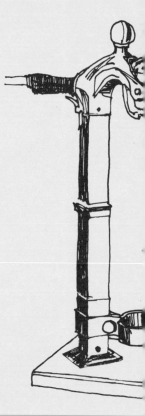

PINEAPPLE ICE CREAM

3 cups crushed pineapple
A vanilla recipe from pages 24 through 35

     Add drained crushed pineapple to vanilla ice cream when it is almost frozen.

MOCHA ALMOND FUDGE

2 cups broken almond nutmeats
1 large can of chocolate sauce
6 T. instant coffee
A vanilla recipe from pages 24 through 35

Dissolve instant coffee in hot mixture when making vanilla ice cream mix. Add nuts before freezing. When removing finished ice cream from cannister, blend sauce through it.

ALMOND ICE CREAM

2 cups broken almond nutmeats
1 T. almond extract
A vanilla recipe from pages 24 through 35

Substitute the almond extract for one tablespoon of vanilla in the vanilla ice cream recipe. Add nuts before freezing.

MARBLE FUDGE ICE CREAM

1 large can chocolate sauce

A vanilla recipe from pages 24 through 35

When ice cream is completed, spoon chocolate sauce through it before placing it in your freezer.

BANANA ICE CREAM

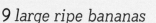

9 *large ripe bananas*

A vanilla recipe from pages 24 through 35

Omit one half of vanilla called for in vanilla ice cream recipe. Force peeled bananas through a sieve and add pulp to ice cream mixture before freezing.

For banana nut ice cream, add two cups of chopped almonds, pecans or walnuts.

8 T. butter
3 cups firmly packed brown sugar
1 1/2 cups chopped pecans
A vanilla recipe from pages 24 through 35

Do not use a custard vanilla as the base for this recipe. Substitute brown sugar for sugar in vanilla recipe. Toast nuts in butter over low heat for 5 minutes. Cool. Add nuts to mix and freeze.

MAPLE ICE CREAM

2 T. maple flavoring
A vanilla recipe from pages 24 through 35

     Substitute maple flavoring for 2 tablespoons of vanilla in vanilla ice cream recipe. For maple nut ice cream, add 2 cups chopped nuts before freezing.

GRAPE ICE CREAM

2 (6 oz.) cans frozen grape juice concentrate
1/2 cup lemon juice
A vanilla recipe from pages 24 through 35

Add lemon juice and grape concentrate to vanilla ice cream before freezing.

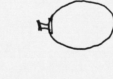

CHOCOLATE CHIP ICE CREAM

2 bags chocolate chips
A vanilla recipe from pages 24 through 35

Chill chocolate chips, then chop as fine as possible. Add to ice cream mix before freezing.

For mocha chip ice cream, add chocolate chips to recipe on page 42.

TOASTED COCONUT ICE CREAM

1T. coconut flavoring

4 cups shredded coconut

A vanilla recipe from pages 24 through 35

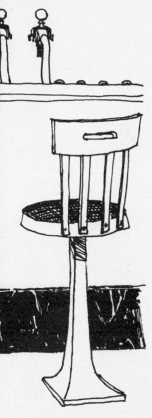

Substitute coconut flavoring for 1 T. of vanilla in ice cream recipe. Toast coconut at 350° in a shallow pan in the oven for 15 minutes, stirring occasionally. Add to the ice cream mixture when partially frozen.

HELPFUL HINTS

The preceding flavored ice cream recipes are the majority of the most popular ice cream flavors normally served in America.

If you would like to make other flavors do not be afraid to try. Here are some hints that may help you. Any fruit may be substituted for the fruits used in the preceding recipes. Just remember to add additional sugar if the fruit needs sweetening. Use the extra space provided in most recipes to change amounts of flavoring to correspond to your own taste buds. For example, after making chocolate ice cream for the first time, you may feel it needs more or less chocolate or sugar. After all, one advantage to making your own ice cream is that you can make it the way you like it.

Try making several flavors at one time. For example, when your vanilla is finished, place it in one quart freezer containers. Spoon chocolate sauce through one quart for Marble Fudge Ice Cream (page 65), and strawberries through one quart for Strawberries and Cream Ice Cream (page 38).

SHERBET

Sherbet is basically a frozen dessert which is made with a fruit juice or puree, a sweetener, and water. Beaten egg white, milk, gelatine or marshmallows are added to this, and this is what makes the difference between sherbet and ices. It gives sherbet a richer, more creamy taste.

Sherbet was originally a French creation made up of fruit juices frozen with liqueurs or wines. Portions were scooped out and sprinkled with more of the same liqueur or wine.

Sherbet is also applied occasionally to describe a sweet fruit drink or a fizzy drink made from sodium bicarbonate, sugar, and tartaric acid.

Because several of the sherbet recipes which follow use egg whites, which are often left over after making custard ice cream, you might consider making one gallon of ice cream and one gallon of sherbert on the same day. You can use the same ice and salt mix for both.

LEMON MILK SHERBET

This is a good way to use some of your egg whites left over from other recipes.

6 egg whites
3/4 cup sugar
3 cups light corn syrup
6 cups whole milk
1 T. grated lemon rind
2 cups lemon juice

Beat egg whites until stiff, but not dry. Gradually beat in sugar, then corn syrup, milk, lemon rind and juice. Chill before putting into canister to freeze.

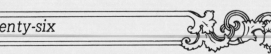

LIME MILK SHERBET

6 egg whites
3/4 cup sugar
3 cups light corn syrup
6 cups whole milk
1 T. grated lime rind
2 cups lime juice

Beat egg whites until stiff, but not dry. Gradually beat in sugar, then corn syrup, milk, lime rind and juice. Chill and freeze.

ORANGE MILK SHERBET

6 egg whites
3/4 cup sugar
3 cups light corn syrup
6 cups whole milk
1 T. grated orange rind
2 cups orange juice

     Beat egg whites until stiff, but not dry. Gradually beat in sugar, then corn syrup, milk, orange rind and juice. Chill and freeze.

STRAWBERRY SHERBET

4 cups water
1 1/2 cups sugar
2 quarts fresh strawberries
1/2 cup lemon juice
2 packages gelatin
4 egg whites

    Mix sugar and water together and boil for about five minutes or until the consistency of light syrup. Pour 1/4 cup of cold water in a bowl and dissolve gelatin in it. Add gelatin to hot syrup. Press berries through a sieve and add lemon juice. Add to syrup mixture. Chill. Beat egg whites stiff, add to chilled mixture and freeze.

ORANGE CREAM SHERBET

This is a creamier sherbet that makes a very rich dessert.

1 cup cold water
4 cups sugar
3 cups hot water
rind from 4 oranges
2 cups lemon juice

3 cups orange juice
1/2 tsp. salt
4 cups cream
2 envelopes powdered gelatine
4 eggs

Grate the orange rind and set aside. Pour the cold water into a bowl and sprinkle the gelatine on top. Add 1 1/2 cups of the sugar and the hot water and stir until dissolved. Then add the orange rind and orange and lemon juices. Put in the canister of the freezer and freeze until mushy. Beat the cream until stiff and add the rest of the sugar and salt. Separate the egg whites from the yolks and beat until stiff. Beat the yolks until thick and lemon colored. Then add both to the cream. Mix with frozen mixture and continue freezing.

ORANGE-LEMON SHERBET

4 1/2 cups sugar
1 1/2 cup orange juice
10 cups milk
3/4 cup lemon juice
1/2 tsp. salt
2 envelopes powdered gelatine

Peel orange and lemon and grate rinds. Squeeze out juice and mix with salt and sugar. Pour a small amount of the milk out into a bowl and sprinkle the gelatine on top. Stir thoroughly and then heat over a double boiler until gelatine dissolves. Then add to the rest of the milk and place in the canister of the freezer.

PINEAPPLE MILK SHERBET

2 cups unsweetened pineapple juice
2 tsp. grated lemon rind
1/2 cup lemon juice

2 cups sugar
1/4 tsp. salt
8 cups cold milk

Stir all the above ingredients together in the milk. Freeze.

PEACH SHERBET

2 cups water
3 cups sugar
4 cups fresh peach pulp
1 cup fresh orange juice
1 cup fresh lemon juice
2 egg whites
1/4 tsp. salt

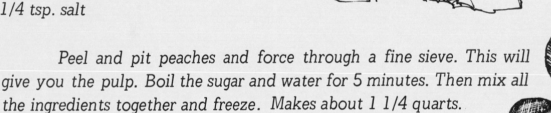

Peel and pit peaches and force through a fine sieve. This will give you the pulp. Boil the sugar and water for 5 minutes. Then mix all the ingredients together and freeze. Makes about 1 1/4 quarts.

GRAPE SHERBET

2 cups cold water
6 cups boiling water
4 cups sugar
1/2 cup lemon juice
2 cans frozen grape juice concentrate
1 cup orange juice
1 tsp. salt
2 envelopes gelatine

Boil the sugar and hot water together for about 5 minutes—until the consistency of light syrup. Pour cold water in a bowl and sprinkle gelatine on top. Combine with syrup and stir until dissolved. Cool slightly and then add the remaining ingredients. Freeze.

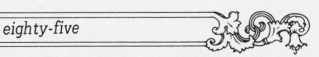

RASPBERRY SHERBET

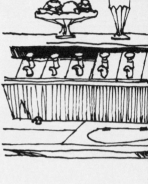

4 cups water
1 1/2 cups sugar
2 quarts fresh raspberries
1/2 cup lemon juice
2 packages gelatine
4 egg whites

Mix the sugar and water together and boil for about 5 minutes until the consistency of syrup. Pour 1/4 cup of the water into a bowl and sprinkle the gelatine on top. Stir until completely dissolved. Then add to the hot syrup. Press raspberries through a sieve and add lemon juice. Add to syrup mixture. Chill. Beat until stiff, but not dry and add the egg whites. Freeze.

STRAWBERRY PINEAPPLE SHERBET

3/4 cup cold water
2 1/2 cups sugar
3 pints fresh strawberries
7 1/2 cups (3 1-pound, 4 ounce cans)
     pineapple juice

1/2 tsp. salt
3 egg whites
2 packages gelatine

Pour water into a bowl and sprinkle gelatine on top. Let stand for 5 minutes. Mix pineapple juice and sugar together and heat until boiling, then stir in the gelatine and chill. Wash the berries, then drain them, mash, and force through a fine sieve. Combine with pineapple mixture, into cannister and partially freeze. Pour into bowl and beat until fluffy. Beat the egg white until stiff and add the salt. Fold this mixture into the sherbet, return to tray and continue freezing until firm.

LEMON-LIME SHERBET

4 cups milk
4 cups light cream
1/2 tsp. salt
1/2 cup sugar
1 1/2 cups (two 6-ounce cans) frozen lemon-
        and-limeade, undiluted
1 envelope unflavored gelatine

Pour 1/2 cup of the milk in a small saucepan and sprinkle gelatine on top. Let stand for 5 minutes. Dissolve over very low heat and mix with remaining ingredients. Chill and then freeze.

GRAPEFRUIT SHERBET

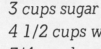

3 cups sugar
4 1/2 cups water
3/4 cup lemon juice
6 cups fresh grapefruit juice
1 cup orange juice
1/2 tsp. salt
6 egg whites
2 packages gelatine

    Put 1 cup of the water in a bowl and add gelatine—stir until dissolved. Boil the sugar and water for about 10 minutes—until the consistency of syrup. Add the gelatine to the surup, and chill. Then mix in the lemon, grapefruit, and orange juices and salt. Beat the egg whites until stiff and add to grapefruit mixture, and freeze.

HOME MADE TOPPINGS

A great favorite with young and old alike is the ice cream sundae. The ice cream parlor with its infinite variety of fancy sundaes which were not only delicious, but were often artistic works are not as common today as they were years ago. However, attractive and delicious sundaes can be made at home and are one of the most appealing desserts that a good host or hostess can serve to guests. The following sundae topping recipes are just a few examples of what can be done. This is an area in which you should let your imagination go to work for you. Don't hesitate to try anything once.

A real treat for a party of youngsters or adults is to put a large variety of sauces and toppings, nuts, cherries and fruits in bowls, along with a big bowl of ice cream, and let all of the guests make their own concoctions.

We have divided the topping section into two parts. First comes home made toppings requiring cooking. These are followed by an easy topping section.

VANILLA SAUCE

1/2 cup sugar
1 T. cornstarch
1 cup boiling water
2 T. butter
1 tsp. vanilla extract
dash of salt

Mix the sugar and cornstarch together in a small saucepan. Stir in the boiling water and simmer for 5 minutes. Stir in the butter and vanilla extract and add salt. Mix well and serve warm. Makes 1 1/4 cups of sauce.

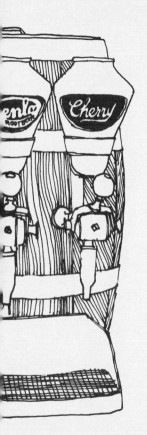

BUTTER SAUCE

1/2 cup butter
1 cup sugar
1/2 cup light cream

Mix all ingredients together and cook until sugar is completely dissolved, stirring constantly. Serve warm.

 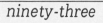

BROWN SUGAR SAUCE

1/3 cup butter or margarine
1/2 cup heavy cream
2 cups firmly packed light brown sugar
1/4 tsp. salt
1/3 cup light corn syrup

Mix all the ingredients together in a saucepan and bring to boil. Cook rapidly for 3 minutes (220° F. on a candy thermometer). Serve warm over ice cream.

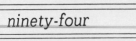

FOAMY SAUCE

1 cup confectioner's (powdered) sugar
1/2 cup soft butter or margarine
2 eggs
1 T. brandy or rum

     Separate the egg yolks from the whites and beat separately. Over a double boiler cream the sugar and butter *together*. Add in the egg yolks and cook over simmering water. Stir constantly until thickened. Fold in the egg whites and brandy or rum. Serve warm. Serves 4 to 6.

HONEY-CREAM SAUCE

1/2 cup honey
1/2 cup light cream
2 T. butter
rum flavoring

Mix together the honey, cream, and butter and cook over low heat for about 10 minutes. Add a little rum flavoring if desired. Makes about 1 cup. Serve warm.

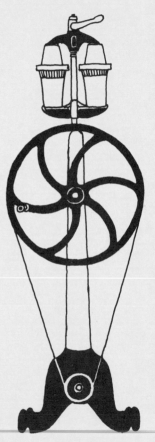

TAFFY SUNDAE SAUCE

3/4 cup butter or margarine
3/4 cup molasses
3/4 cup sugar
3/4 cup diluted evaporated milk
1 1/2 tsp. vanilla extract
1 cup pecans

Melt the butter over a very low heat and add in the sugar and molasses. Bring all to a rapid boil then reduce the heat and boil for 2 minutes, stirring constantly to prevent burning. Remove from heat and cool slightly. Stir in the remaining ingredients. Serve hot or cold over your favorite vanilla ice cream. Makes about 2 1/2 cups.

MARSHMALLOW SAUCE

1/2 lb. marshmallows
1/2 cup orange juice
1 T. maraschino juice
2 cups sugar
2/3 cup water
3 egg whites

Mix the orange juice and maraschino together. Cut the marshmallows into small pieces and soak in the orange juice mixture. Combine the sugar and water and cook until the consistency of syrup. Then beat the egg whites and pour the syrup slowly on top. Beat until creamy, and cool. When cooled, add the marshmallows.

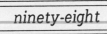

CUSTARD SAUCE

1 1/2 cups milk
3 egg yolks
3 T. sugar
1/8 tsp. salt
vanilla or almond extract

Heat the milk to boiling point in a double boiler over simmering water. Mix together the egg yolks, sugar, and salt. Stir in a small amount of hot milk then return all to the remaining milk in the double boiler. Cook, stirring constantly, until thickened. Cool. Flavor sauce with vanilla or almond extract. A little lemon rind may also be added if desired. Makes about 1 3/4 cups.

4 egg yolks, slightly beaten
1/4 cup sugar
1/8 tsp. salt
2 oz. (2 squares) unsweetened chocolate
2 cups milk
1/2 tsp. vanilla extract

Add the sugar and salt to the beaten egg yolks and mix together well. Melt the chocolate in the milk, stirring constantly, then beat to blend. Stir this into the egg mixture. Cook in a double boiler over simmering water, stirring constantly, until the mixture thickens. Add the vanilla, cool, and chill. Makes about 2 1/2 cups.

CHOCOLATE SAUCE

2 oz. (2 squares) unsweetened chocolate
3/4 cup milk
1 1/2 cups sugar
3 T. light corn syrup
1/4 tsp. salt
2 T. butter
1 tsp. vanilla extract

　　　Melt the chocolate in the milk in a saucepan over very low heat. Stir constantly. When chocolate is completely melted and blended in, beat until smooth. Add the sugar, corn syrup and salt. Cook for 2 or 3 minutes, stirring occasionally. Add the butter and vanilla. Makes 2 cups.

BITTERSWEET-CHOCOLATE SAUCE

8 oz. (8 squares) unsweetened chocolate
2 cups sugar
1 can (14 1/2 oz.) evaporated milk, undiluted
2 T. strong black coffee
dash of salt
1 tsp. vanilla extract

Melt the chocolate in a double boiler over boiling water. Add in the sugar and blend well. Cook, covered, over boiling water for 30 minutes. Add the evaporated milk, coffee, salt and vanilla and beat until smooth and thick. This sauce should be served hot. It can be made ahead of time and kept in the refrigerator for several weeks. To reheat, simply put in the double boiler over boiling water. Makes about 3 cups.

HOT CARAMEL SAUCE

1 1/2 cups sugar
1/2 cup light corn syrup
6 T. butter
1 cup light cream
1/2 tsp. salt
1/2 tsp. vanilla extract

Mix together in a saucepan the sugar, corn syrup, 3 tablespoons of the butter, and 1/2 cup of the cream. Bring to a boil and gradually add the remaining butter and cream. Cook over medium heat, stirring occasionally, until thickened. Remove from heat and add the salt and vanilla. Serve warm. To reheat, simply put sauce in a double boiler over simmering water. Makes 1 3/4 cups.

HOT FUDGE SAUCE

1 cup sugar
2 T. flour
1/2 tsp. salt
1 cup water
2 oz. (2 squares) unsweetened chocolate
2 T. butter
1 tsp. vanilla extract

Combine the sugar, flour, and salt in a saucepan and blend in the water. Add the chocolate and cook over medium heat, stirring constantly until the mixture boils. Remove from the heat and blend in the butter and vanilla extract. Serve hot over creamy vanilla ice cream.

BUTTERSCOTCH SAUCE

1/2 cup light corn syrup
1/3 cup butter or margarine
1 1/2 cups firmly packed brown sugar
2/3 cup light cream

Combine the corn syrup, butter, and brown sugar in a saucepan and cook, stirring occasionally, over medium heat until thickened. Cool for about 5 minutes then blend in the cream. Serve hot or cold. Makes 2 1/4 cups.

NUT-FUDGE SAUCE

2 cups sugar
1 cup brown sugar
3 oz. (3 squares) unsweetened chocolate
3/4 cup cream
2 T. butter
1 tsp. vanilla
1 cup chopped nuts

Mix together in a saucepan the sugar, brown sugar, chocolate, cream, and butter. Cook over medium heat until the mixture crinkles around the edge of the saucepan. Remove from the heat and add the vanilla and chopped nuts. Serve at once.

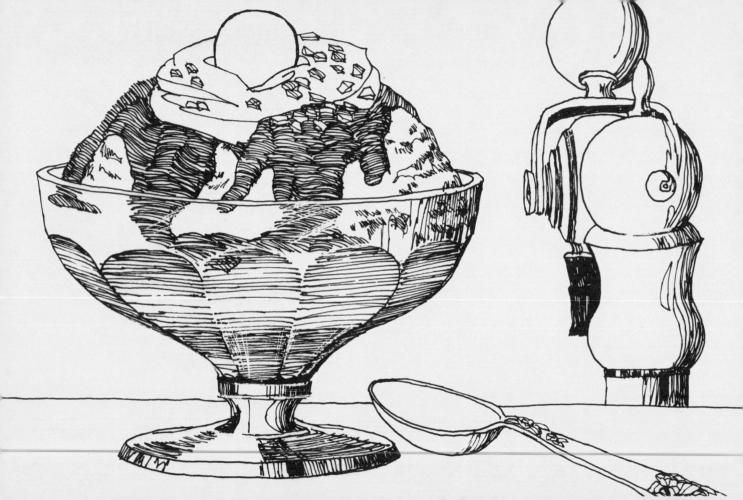

EASY SUNDAES

On the pages that follow are recipes for quick and easy sundaes that you can make in a few minutes with foodstuffs that are readily available in your kitchen or nearby store.

Don't limit yourself to vanilla ice cream when making sundaes. Try these toppings with several different kinds of ice cream, and don't hesitate to use two types of ice creams with two different toppings.

One last word, don't forget the whipped cream, chopped nuts and cherry to top off your sundaes. They add the crowning touch to your home made creations.

ORANGE-BLUEBERRY SUNDAE

Garnish two scoops of peach ice cream with equal amounts of orange segments, sliced bananas, and blueberries.

STOP-AND-GO SUNDAE

Combine chopped green and red maraschino cherries and add a little light corn syrup. Pour over vanilla or cherry ice cream.

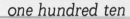

HOT CARAMEL SUNDAE

Add 2 T. water to 1/2 lb. of caramels and melt down to a thick syrup over hot water. Top with nuts if desired.

ORIENTAL SUNDAE

Cut up into small pieces a couple of undrained preserved kumquats. Spoon over chocolate ice cream.

PEACH SUNDAE

Slice up frozen or sweetened fresh peaches and serve over rich French Vanilla ice cream.

PINK SUNDAE

Spoon 1 or 2 T. grenadine over vanilla ice cream—top with a sprig of mint.

PINEAPPLE SUNDAE

Spoon some canned crushed pineapple over vanilla or banana ice cream, include a little juice as well.

TART ORANGE SUNDAE

Pour canned frozen orange juice concentrate over chocolate or vanilla ice cream.

EASY SUNDAES

PARTY ORANGE SUNDAE

3 very large oranges　　　　1 banana
1 cup strawberries　　　　　1 pint orange sherbet

Cut the oranges in half and neatly scoop out the orange segments. Slice the banana and combine with the strawberries and orange segments. Place a scoop of sherbet in each orange shell and top with the fruit. Serve immediately. Serves 6. Grapefruit can be substituted for the orange if desired.

MARSHMALLOW SUNDAE

You can either buy ready-made marshmallow cream or make your own by melting down marshmallows slowly in a double boiler. Best on chocolate, peach, and pineapple ice creams.

EASY SUNDAES

MOLASSES CHIP SUNDAE

Sprinkle some crushed molasses chips over vanilla, chocolate, or banana ice cream.

MOCHA SUNDAE

Mix powdered instant coffee with your favorite chocolate syrup and pour over chocolate or vanilla or coffee ice cream.

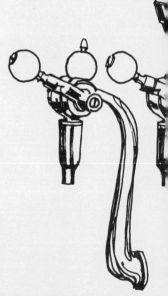

MINCEMEAT SUNDAE

Mix a little rum or brandy in with the mincemeat. Serve warm over vanilla ice cream—great at Christmas time.

RUM-MANGO SUNDAE

1 large ripe mango
1/3 cup rum
1/4 cup sugar
vanilla ice cream

Peel the mango and slice it into thin slices (about 1/4 inch). Put into a shallow dish and sprinkle the sugar and rum on top. Refrigerate for 1 hour before serving. When chilled and ready to serve, spoon over vanilla or mango ice cream. Serves 4.

JAM SUNDAE

Serve your favorite jam over ice cream. Cherry, plum, apricot, and any berry jams are delicious.

EASY SUNDAES

MAPLE-RUM SUNDAE

Heat up as much maple syrup as you will use in a double boiler. Flavor it with a little rum or rum extract and serve over coffee or your favorite nut ice cream.

GINGER SUNDAE

Pour ginger marmalade or chopped preserved ginger root in syrup over vanilla ice cream.

MARMALADE SUNDAE

Top vanilla ice cream with your favorite marmalade.

one hundred seventeen

EASY SUNDAES

CANDIED FRUIT SUNDAE

Spoon moist mixed candied fruits over vanilla or pistachio ice cream.

DESERT SUNDAE

Moisten chopped fresh dates with honey and serve over butter-pecan or burnt-almond ice cream.

TROPICAL SUNDAE

Combine chopped coconut, white raisins, and chopped walnuts to butterscotch sauce and pour over ice cream.

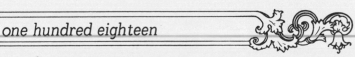

BRANDIED FRUIT SUNDAE

Cut up a quantity of brandied fruit and serve over coffee, pineapple, coconut, banana, or vanilla ice cream.

COOKIE SUNDAE

Top your favorite ice cream with crushed fig cookies, coconut bars, or macaroons.

PEANUT BRITTLE SUNDAE

Sprinkle crushed peanut brittle over vanilla, chocolate, coffee, or caramel ice cream.

EASY SUNDAES

LIQUEUR SUNDAE

Top your favorite ice cream with Cointreau, crème de menthe, or any liqueur.

PINEAPPLE-GINGER SUNDAE

Mix in a small amount of chopped candied ginger root to pineapple jam and serve over vanilla ice cream.

CHOCOLATE-RUM SUNDAE

Melt down chocolate rum wafers in a double boiler over hot water and serve over vanilla or chocolate ice cream.

BLACK AND WHITE SUNDAE

Use one scoop of vanilla ice cream and one scoop of chocolate. Cover the chocolate with marshmallow sauce and vanilla with chocolate sauce. Add whipped cream, cherries and nuts.

COCONUT SUNDAE

Roll balls of your favorite ice cream in shredded coconut and top with your favorite sauce.

EASY SUNDAES

FLAVORED WHIPPED CREAM TOPPINGS

1 1/2 cups heavy cream   1/8 tsp. salt
1/2 cup sugar   1/2 tsp. vanilla extract

Before whipping, add one of the following to the basic recipe above to make a delicious thick, creamy topping.

Instant coffee powder
Instant cocoa mix   Brown sugar instead of granulated sugar
Any flavoring extract   Quick strawberry-flavored beverage mix

Or, one of the following can be folded into the whipped cream.

Chopped nuts
Macaroon crumbs   Chopped raisins
Chocolate sprinkles   Grenadine instead of sugar

BANANA SPLIT

One ripe banana
1 scoop each of vanilla, chocolate, and strawberry ice cream
2 T. strawberry preserves
2 T. of pineapple preserves
2 T. of chocolate sauce
Whipped cream
2 T. of chopped nuts
1 maraschino cherry

Split the banana into halves lengthwise. Arrange ice cream scoops in a row between banana halves. Spoon strawberry preserves over one scoop, pineapple over another and chocolate sauce over the last. Top with whipped cream and garnish with nuts and cherry.

OTHER CONCOCTIONS

The ways in which ice cream can be used for delightful desserts and snacks is probably infinite.

On the pages which follow, we cover many of the more popular ice cream concoctions in use today.

If you keep the ingredients on hand, and if you always have your own delicious home made ice cream in the freezer, you can serve super desserts that will be the delight of your family and guests with very little effort on your part . . . . . . and when you use the rich custard and cream varieties of ice cream, you'll be creating desserts which will rival those served to royalty.

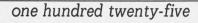

ICE CREAM SODAS

Sodas are easy to make. First take a small amount of vanilla ice cream and blend it thoroughly with the syrup in the bottom of the glass before adding the carbonated water. This way, you are first creating a flavored soda water. Then add a large scoop of vanilla ice cream. Top with whipped cream and a cherry.

For more flavorful sodas try using flavored ice creams. For example, use strawberry ice cream in strawberry sodas, banana ice cream in banana sodas and so on. Just remember to first mix some of the ice cream with the syrup to create the base.

FLOATS

Floats are made with flavored soda water and vanilla ice cream. All you have to do is fill a large glass with root beer, cola, or any other flavored soda water and then add a large scoop of vanilla ice cream. The root beer float is the all-time favorite.

The freeze is a sherbet soda. First mix a small amount of sherbet with the syrup in the bottom of the glass. Use lemon, lime, or orange syrup with the same flavor of sherbet. Then add carbonated water and top off with a large scoop of sherbet. You can stop there if you wish, or you can carefully spoon additional sherbet around the top of the glass and top it off with whipped cream and a cherry. This is a wonderful thirst quencher for a hot day.

MILK SHAKES AND MALTS

If you like thin milk shakes, you can use a egg beater, blender or electric mixer. Simply place 1/2 cup milk, 2 scoops of ice cream, and your favorite syrup in any of the above and mix. For malts, add 1 tablespoon malted milk. You will soon have a conventional shake.

If you like thick milk shakes, you can't use an egg beater or electirc mixer. You must use a blender or a milk shake mixer. Use the same proportions as above and then keep adding ice cream until it is thick enough to suit you.

The home made ice cream milk shake is so good that you'll never want any other kind.

FROSTEDS

Frosteds are super sodas. First mix syrup with a small amount of ice cream and then add soda water to fill the glass. Carefully spoon several spoonfuls of the same flavor of ice cream as the syrup around the top of the glass to make a cover for the glass. Then spoon vanilla ice cream on top of it and finish it off with whipped cream and a cherry. What you have done is covered the soda. It is frosted.

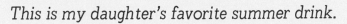

This is my daughter's favorite summer drink.

3/4 cup freshly squeezed orange juice,
    or frozen orange juice
1 T. lemon juice
6 or 7 scoops of orange sherbet

    Put all the ingredients in the blender. Blend until almost smooth but still thick. Pour into tall glasses and top with a cherry. Makes 2 average sized servings.

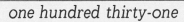

MERINGUE ICE CREAM CUPS

1 egg white
1/3 cup sugar
1/2 tsp. vanilla
1/3 cup chopped pecans
3 soda crackers, crushed

Beat the egg white in a mixing bowl until soft peaks form. Add the sugar and vanilla gradually until stiff peaks form. Stir in the pecans and crackers. Spread a rounded teaspoonful of the mixture on the bottom and sides of 6 well-buttered muffin cups. Bake at 325° for 25 to 30 minutes until light golden brown. Cool about 5 minutes. To remove from the cups, carefully loosen the edges with a paring knife.

These cups, when cooled, can be filled with any combination of ice cream, syrup, or fresh fruit, etc.

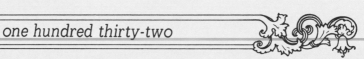

CHERRIES JUBILEE

2 T. butter
2 T. sugar   1/4 cup lemon juice
1 tsp. grated orange rind   1/4 cup Kirsch
1 tsp. grated lemon rind   3 cups canned bing cherries, pitted and drained
1/4 cup orange juice   1/4 cup warm brandy

In a chafing dish melt the butter over high heat. Blend in the sugar, mix well, and heat until the mixture bubbles. Stir in orange and lemon rinds and simmer until the mixture is light brown. Stir in orange and lemon juices and cook until mixture bubbles again. Add Kirsch and cherries. Stir until the cherries are well saturated. Pour in the warm brandy, light it, and stir the sauce until the flames die away. Serve over vanilla ice cream.

BAKED ALASKA

1 cup sifted all-purpose flour
2/3 cup sugar
1/4 cup shortening
1/2 cup milk
1 1/2 tsp. baking powder

1/2 tsp. salt
1 tsp. vanilla extract
1 egg
1 quart brick ice cream
meringue

Grease and flour lightly a 9-inch square pan. Sift together the flour, sugar, baking powder and salt in a mixing bowl. Add the shortening and milk. Beat 1 1/2 minutes with a mixer on low speed or 225 strokes by hand. Add in the egg and vanilla and beat for another 1 1/2 minutes. Pour into pan and bake at 350° for 20 to 25 minutes, or until a toothpick inserted into cake comes out clean. Cool. Place cake on a cookie sheet and cut strips 2 inches wide from each side of cake. Put

ice cream on top of cake and completely cover both with meringue. Seal meringue to edges. Bake at 450° for 5 minutes, or until lightly browned. Serve at once.

MERINGUE TOPPING

8 egg whites at room temperature
pinch of salt
3/4 cup superfine sugar

Beat the egg whites and salt until they form soft peaks. Still beating, slowly pour in the sugar and continue to beat for about 5 minutes, until the egg whites are stiff and glossy. Immediately spread over cake and ice cream.

ICE CREAM BONBONS

1 quart ice cream
2 cups chopped pecans or other nuts   1/2 cup margarine
12 onces semi-sweet chocolate pieces   1 T. instant coffee powder

Make your ice cream balls with a large melon ball scoop. Roll each ball in nuts immediately and put in freezer until completely frozen, at least 1 hour. Melt the chocolate and margarine in a double boiler over hot water. Mix in the coffee. Take away from heat but keep warm over hot water. Using a fork, dip the ice cream balls into the chocolate-coffee mixture, working as quickly as possible. Dip sets of 10 or 12 at a time, then return to freezer and continue. When the chocolate is set completely, put the bonbons in paper cups, 3 or 4 to a serving. Cover or wrap with foil or plastic wrap and store in your freezer until ready to serve. Makes 30 to 36 bonbons.

PARFAIT

Parfait is a French word meaning "perfect." A phrase used by many to describe this dish. American parfaits consist of ice cream served with whipped cream, fruit, or other sauces piled in layers in a tall, narrow glass called a "parfait glass." It is often topped with sweet whipped cream and garnished with a maraschino cherry.

In a parfait glass or juice glass, alternate layers of ice cream with jam, syrup, baby or junior fruit, or marshmallow cream. Here are some good combinations you can use:

—Strawberry ice cream and strawberry jam
—Vanilla ice cream and red raspberry jam
—Cherry ice cream and almond-flavored whipped cream

PARFAIT

—Vanilla ice cream with apricot and apple, or pear and pineapple baby or junior fruit
—Chocolate ice cream and marshmallow cream

Any combination of ice cream and sauce that strikes your fancy can be tried, and can't help but be delicious!

PRINCE PÜCKLER'S BOMBE

This spherical three-layered ice cream dessert was named after a noted Prussian cook and gourmet, Hermann von Pückler-Muskau.

3 T. rum
2 cups coarsely crushed macaroons
1 quart chocolate ice cream
1 pint vanilla ice cream
1 pint strawberry ice cream or raspberry sherbet
1 cup heavy cream, whipped, sweetened, and
   flavored with vanilla extract
fresh strawberries or shaved chocolate

Chill a 6-cup fluted bombe mold for 1 hour. Sprinkle rum over macaroon crumbs. Stir and let stand about one hour. Soften the

PRINCE PUCKLER'S BOMBE

chocolate ice cream slightly—until it can be pressed into the mold. Do not let it melt into a liquid. Pack firmly into the bottom of the mold and well into the sides. Sprinkle with a layer of 1/3 of the macaroon crumbs. Cover the mold and freeze until the crumbs and ice cream are hard. Let the vanilla ice cream soften and pack it into the mold, top with half of the remaining crumbs. Cover the mold and freeze again. Repeat with the strawberry ice cream and the rest of the crumbs. Cover the mold and freeze for 6 to 8 hours or until the ice cream is very hard. Unmold and slice in long wedges to serve. Serve plain or garnish with whipped cream and fresh strawberries or shaved chocolate. Serves 12.

BROWNIE ICE CREAM SANDWICHES

1 pint of your favorite ice cream, softened
1 package fudge brownie mix

Prepare and bake brownie mix as directed and cool. Cut through the center to make two halves. Spread ice cream between the layers and wrap in foil paper. Freeze until firm, about 2 to 3 hours. Remove from freezer a few minutes before serving. Cut into 1-inch slices and serve immediately. Refreeze unused slices. Makes 8 to 10 sandwiches.

INDEX

NOTES

NOTES

 NOTES

 NOTES

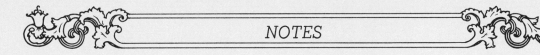

NOTES

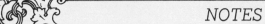

NOTES